NAVIGATING THE WA: HOW TO THRIVE IN JAPAN'S COLLABORATIVE WORK CULTURE

BY

Brian Takahashi

TABLE OF CONTENTS

Introduction

Hi there, I'm Brian. I want to be upfront with you about working in Japan. It is not easy to point out all the areas of contention between cultures without sounding cynical or hypercritical. Please note that I enjoy where I am in life and have a loving family and a wonderful community where I live in. I have been living and working in Japan for 11 years, am married to my Japanese wife, have two children, and have worked in both the public and private sectors in full and part-time employment.

The majority of my experience in Japan is that of English Language Education. If you want to become an ALT (Assistant Language Teacher), this is the book to read. If you aren't seeking English Language Education, the reader will still have the vast majority of information necessary to understand what working for a company would be like.

Japan is a great place to work, but it is best to challenge any pop culture misconceptions about how things are in Japan. There are many. I ask that you keep an open mind as most pop culture bits consumed online and elsewhere tend to be from the tourist's perspective, not the employees. The two have vast differences; you should know this before coming to Japan. Understanding these misconceptions will likely lessen the blow of culture shock, which usually sets in within the first 2-6 months of living in the country. And for many, it is a "make or break" moment that generally decides whether they resign for another contract the following year.

Knowing what to expect before you start may allow you to have a long and lasting career in Japan and find fulfillment in whichever employment you seek. Whether you are looking to work for a year abroad or have decided to become a lifer (term by those of us that have started families here), this guide will help you gain insight into some of the significant aspects of employment in Japan.

Before we dive right into this, it is essential to note that Japanese work culture and societal norms have many areas that overlap. So, if I say "culture," I am likely referring to aspects of Japanese social interactions, and if I say "work culture," I am referring to something that will only occur at your place of employment.

PART I: Understanding Societal Aspects Of Japan

Chapter One: The Wa, Harmony, and Collaboration

If you're a foreigner looking to work in Japan, you may have heard of "The Wa." This Japanese concept refers to harmony, balance, and unity in all aspects of life. Understanding and respecting The Wa is essential for anyone looking to succeed in the Japanese workplace, and it can also help you navigate Japanese society as a whole. In this guide, we'll explore what The Wa means, how it applies to the workplace, and how you can cultivate it to improve your chances of success.

First, let's delve a little deeper into what The Wa means. At its core, The Wa is about finding balance and harmony in all aspects of life. This balance can manifest in many ways, from how people interact with one another to how they approach work and other obligations. In the Japanese workplace, The Wa is reflected in the emphasis on teamwork, collaboration, and consensus building. Rather than focusing on individual achievement, the Japanese prioritize the collective good, with the understanding that everyone benefits when the team succeeds.

When looking to succeed in the Japanese workplace, it's crucial to understand and respect The Wa. This respect means being mindful of others, putting the team's needs above your own, and working towards consensus rather than pushing your agenda. It also means being patient, respectful, and open-minded, even when disagreeing with your colleagues. By cultivating these qualities, you can become a valued team member and earn your Japanese colleagues' trust and respect.

One fundamental way to cultivate The Wa is through communication. In the Japanese workplace, contact is often indirect and implicit, with much left unsaid. Indirect communication can be challenging for foreigners, who may be more accustomed to direct communication styles. However, by paying close attention to nonverbal cues, reading between the lines, and being attuned to the overall tone of the conversation, you can begin to pick up on the nuances of Japanese communication. Working on your indirect communication will enable you to communicate more effectively with your colleagues, build stronger relationships, and ultimately succeed in the workplace.

Another important aspect of The Wa is respect for hierarchy and authority. In Japan, there is a strong emphasis on respecting one's superiors, which is reflected in the workplace. If you're working in Japan, it's essential to be mindful of the company hierarchy, defers to those in positions of authority, and show respect for those with more experience or seniority. The most common signs of respect involve bowing, using honorific language, or engaging in other forms of deference. Doing so can demonstrate your adherence to The Wa and commitment to the team.

Finally, it's worth noting that The Wa is not just about work - it applies to all aspects of life in Japan. Whether navigating social situations, interacting with neighbors, or simply going about your daily life, it's essential to be mindful of The Wa and strive for harmony and balance. Things that help maintain the Wa include being quiet and reserved in public spaces, not disturbing others, or respecting local customs and traditions. Doing so can demonstrate your respect for Japanese culture and build stronger relationships with the people around you.

The Wa is a crucial concept for anyone looking to work in Japan. By understanding and respecting this idea of harmony, balance, and unity, you can become a valued team member, earn the trust and respect of your Japanese colleagues, and ultimately succeed in the workplace. By cultivating qualities such as patience, respect, and open-mindedness, paying close attention to communication, and showing deference to those in positions of authority, you can demonstrate your commitment to The Wa and the collective good. Whether you're working in Japan for a short time or planning to make a long-term commitment, embracing The Wa is essential for not only succeeding in the workplace, building meaningful relationships, and thriving in Japanese society as a whole. Remember, The Wa is not just a concept for the workplace - it applies to all aspects of life in Japan. By embodying The Wa in your everyday interactions, you can show respect for Japanese culture and customs and build deeper connections with the people around you. With patience, persistence, and a commitment to harmony and balance, you can make the most of your experience working in Japan and create a fulfilling and rewarding life.

Chapter Two: How Japanese Collectivism Works

This idea is deeply ingrained in Japanese society and culture and can significantly impact the workplace. In this guide, we'll explore what Japanese collectivism means, how it affects the workplace, and how you can cultivate a collectivist mindset to succeed in Japan.

At its core, Japanese collectivism is about valuing the group over the individual. In Japan, there is a strong emphasis on cooperation, teamwork, and consensus building. Rather than focusing on individual achievement, the Japanese prioritize the collective good, with the understanding that everyone benefits when the team succeeds. Collaborative thinking can be a significant adjustment for foreigners, especially those from cultures that prioritize individualism.

Understanding and respecting Japanese collectivism means being mindful of others, putting the team's needs above your own, and working towards consensus rather than pushing your agenda. It also means being patient, respectful, and open-minded, even when disagreeing with your colleagues. By cultivating these qualities, you can become a valued team member and earn your Japanese colleagues' trust and respect.

One fundamental way to cultivate a collectivist mindset is through communication. In the Japanese workplace, communication is often indirect and implicit, with much left unsaid. However, by paying close attention to nonverbal cues, reading between the lines, and being attuned to the overall tone of the conversation, you can begin to pick up on the nuances of Japanese communication. These tactics will enable you to communicate more effectively with your colleagues, build stronger relationships, and ultimately succeed in the workplace.

Finally, it's worth noting that Japanese collectivism is not just about work - it applies to all aspects of life in Japan. Whether navigating social situations, interacting with neighbors, or simply going about your daily life, it's essential to be mindful of Japanese collectivism and strive for cooperation, teamwork, and consensus building.

Japanese collectivism is a crucial concept for anyone looking to work in Japan. By understanding and respecting this idea of valuing the group over the individual, you can become a valued team member, earn the trust and respect of your Japanese colleagues, and ultimately succeed in the workplace. By cultivating qualities such as patience, respect, and open-mindedness, paying close attention to communication, and showing deference to those in positions of authority, you can demonstrate your commitment to Japanese collectivism and the collective good. Whether working in Japan for a short time or planning to make a long-term commitment, embracing Japanese collectivism is essential for succeeding in the workplace, building meaningful relationships, and thriving in Japanese society.

Chapter Three: Why Perception is More Important Than the Truth

In Japan, the perception of self-image is heavily influenced by the concept of "honne" and "tatemae." Honne refers to a person's true feelings and opinions, while tatemae refers to the public face that a person presents to others. In Japanese culture, expressing your honne in public is considered impolite; instead, people are expected to give a positive tatemae. This facade means that, in the workplace, it's essential to cultivate a positive self-image that aligns with the expectations of Japanese society. If there are three boxes to carry upstairs, five people may go down together to take boxes. Three will move them, and two will walk back empty-handed, but the group will get the credit and a good Perception of teamwork.

One key aspect of cultivating a positive self-image in Japan is appearance. In Japanese culture, appearance plays a significant role in how others perceive a person. Maintaining this appearance means paying close attention to grooming, dressing professionally, and maintaining appropriate formality in your attire. Conservative attire can be challenging for foreigners who may be more accustomed to casual workplace attire. Still, dressing conservatively demonstrates your respect for Japanese culture and shows your commitment to presenting a positive self-image.

Looking around your office, you will notice trends; following them to "group" yourself with the rest of your colleagues is best. They may even comment nicely on your "haircut" or "is that a new suit" as long as it is within the group's norms. So if you work in an office and are a man, you'll be expected at a bare minimum to wear a light-colored (shade of white, grey, or blue) shirt with a tie and dress pants/trousers. Most men wear full suits from October to May. Depending on your office rules on "shoes in the office," you will most likely wear dress shoes. For women, you will be expected to wear skirts and dresses, no open-toe shoes and likely heels, and all tops must cover cleavage. You will also be expected to put on makeup (just base foundation and mascara will be OK). And while you are freer to choose colors than men, try not to wear "bright" clothing. Bright pinks, oranges, greens, and reds will cause you to stand out, especially to those older than you in your group.

It's also worth noting that, in Japan, there is a strong emphasis on (kuki-yomu) "reading the air." Reading the air means being attuned to nonverbal cues, such as body language and facial expressions, to understand the mood and tone of a situation.

Another important aspect of cultivating a positive self-image in Japan is language. In Japanese culture, language plays a significant role in how others perceive a person. Acquiring a positive self-image through language means paying close attention to your language use, using honorifics appropriately, and being mindful of your tone and intonation. By doing so, you can demonstrate your respect for Japanese culture and show your colleagues that you are a professional who takes your work seriously.

Finally, it's important to remember that cultivating a positive self-image in Japan is not just about the workplace - it applies to all aspects of life in Japan. Whether interacting with colleagues, navigating social situations, or simply going about your daily life, it's essential to be mindful of Japanese culture and strive to present a positive self-image that aligns with society's expectations. By doing so, you can build stronger relationships, earn the respect of others, and ultimately succeed in Japan.

Perception of self-image is a crucial concept for anyone looking to work in Japan. By understanding and respecting the Japanese perception of self-image and cultivating a positive self-image that aligns with society's expectations, you can become a valued team member, earn the trust and respect of your Japanese colleagues, and ultimately succeed in the workplace. By paying close attention to appearance, behavior, language, and nonverbal cues and striving to present a positive self-image in all aspects of your life in Japan, you can demonstrate your respect for Japanese culture and build meaningful relationships with the people around you.

Remember, perception is everything in Japan, and by presenting yourself positively and respectfully, you can create a solid first impression that can pave the way for long-term success. It's also important to be patient and open-minded, as cultural differences can take time to understand and navigate. By approaching new experiences with an open mind and a willingness to learn, you can show your Japanese colleagues that you are committed to building positive relationships and contributing to the team. Ultimately, cultivating a positive self-image and demonstrating your respect for Japanese culture, you can thrive in the workplace and achieve your goals in Japan.

Now let's try to make this more practical and give you a more in-depth understanding of perception with some examples. In Japan, your colleagues, neighbors, acquaintances, and superiors' perception of you; is how people see you in Japanese culture. The truth is irrelevant. For instance, if you come to work one day with a monotone voice, speak to no one, and come across as hard and strict, everyone assumes you are always this way and will treat you like this. They may not know you happily teach small children on weekends at the community center, that you are part of a comedy troop, or even that you volunteer at a soup kitchen. That is irrelevant because of how you were perceived on that one day. When you interact with colleagues, you need to see whether or not they are putting on their "perception" or natural face. Most Japanese people you meet may never show you their "real" look. There are even times when my wife uses her perception face with me in daily interactions. Though I have seen her natural face, understanding both is essential to understanding everyday life in Japan.

Much frustration is brought on these people because they didn't understand the social norms inside Japan before they got there. If you are looking to assimilate into Japanese society, you should ask yourself three questions about everything you do:

1. Is there anything contentious in what I am about to say?
2. What can and will the people in my immediate surrounding think?
3. How opinionated is what I am about to say?
As funny as it may sound, this is what goes through the minds of your colleagues before any interaction they have with you.

Chapter Four: Honne and Tatemae How to Say What You Mean Without Meaning What You Say

One of the most important concepts to understand is the idea of honne and tatemae. These two concepts are deeply ingrained in Japanese culture and significantly impact communication, relationships, and social dynamics. Understanding and respecting honne and tatemae can build strong relationships with your Japanese colleagues, avoid misunderstandings and conflicts, and ultimately succeed in the workplace.

Honne refers to a person's true feelings, thoughts, and intentions. In other words, it is what a person feels or thinks about a particular situation or person. Tatemae, on the other hand, refers to the public face or facade that a person presents to the world. It is the behavior, language, and attitudes that a person uses to conform to social norms and expectations. In many cases, tatemae may be at odds with a person's honne, as Japanese society strongly emphasizes maintaining harmony and avoiding conflict.

As a foreigner working in Japan, it can be easy to understand or interpret the behavior of your Japanese colleagues. It is complicated and particularly true regarding honne and tatemae, as Japanese people may only sometimes express their true feelings or intentions directly.

Because confrontation is avoided and polite behavior is critical, you may engage in a conversation where you think the topic is of mutual interest when it is feigned politeness. The person you spoke with may take extra steps to avoid talking with you though every time you meet, they smile and seem genuinely interested. This confusion is why many people who have lived in Japan without understanding this say, "Japanese people are liars." Japanese people aren't liars; their communication style is just different. However, paying close attention to verbal and nonverbal cues, you can understand the difference between honne and tatemae and navigate social situations more effectively.

One of the critical aspects of honne and tatemae is the importance of indirect communication. Because collectivism in Japan requires people to work in groups, and being against the group can lead to ostracization, confrontation is avoided like the plague. Seeming confrontational or even just levying a point of criticism could be viewed as "anti-group" behavior. The facade of tatemae is why when people say Japan is a polite society, they are correct and wrong at the same time. Many are polite out of fear of being ostracized from the group without their true intentions being made known.

In Japanese culture, confrontation or criticism can damage relationships. Instead, Japanese people often use indirect language or hints to express their feelings. For example, if a colleague is unhappy with your work, they may say something like, "that's an interesting approach," or "let's consider some other options." While these statements may seem neutral, they may indicate dissatisfaction or disagreement.

By paying close attention to verbal and nonverbal cues, you can begin to understand the difference between honne and tatemae and avoid misunderstandings. For example, if a colleague appears tense or avoids eye contact, it may indicate they are uncomfortable with the situation or disagree with your approach. Similarly, if a colleague expresses disagreement indirectly, it may be a sign that they are unhappy with your work.

So, in your daily interactions, your words are monitored by the group, and your facial expressions and body language. As mentioned earlier, the assumptions created by those dictate how you are perceived, and as I explained before, perception is more important than the actual truth.

As a foreigner working in Japan, it's essential to understand and respect these cultural norms. Using the cultural norms may mean adopting a more indirect communication style, showing deference to those in positions of authority, and prioritizing the group's needs over your desires. Respecting these cultural norms can build strong relationships with your Japanese colleagues and contribute to a positive and harmonious work environment.

Understanding honne and tatemae is essential for any foreigner looking to work in Japan. By paying close attention to verbal and nonverbal cues, adopting an indirect communication style, and respecting group harmony and consensus-building, you can build strong relationships with your Japanese colleagues and thrive in the workplace.

If you wish to understand this further, I highly recommend reading my book *"Cracking the Code: Honne and Tatemae in Japan"* for a more in-depth understanding.

Chapter Five: Don't Stick Out. Why The Tallest Nail Gets Hammered First

In Japanese business culture, a proverb goes, "The tallest nail is hammered first." At first glance, this has significant implications for anyone looking to work in Japan. In essence, the proverb means that those who stick out or draw too much attention to themselves are likely to be targeted or criticized. To avoid this fate, blending in with the group and avoiding standing out too much is often better.

Understanding the proverb "The tallest nail is hammered first" is essential for a foreigner who wants to work in Japan. Japanese society is highly collectivistic, and individuals are expected to prioritize the group's well-being over their interests. This principle applies to the workplace as well. In a Japanese office, employees are expected to work collaboratively towards a common goal. Those who disrupt this harmony by standing out or drawing too much attention to themselves may be viewed negatively. If you throw your opinion out first, in front of everyone at a meeting, one of two things will happen:

A. (<1% chance) Your boss will like your proposal and implement it immediately.

B. (>99% chance) Your boss will criticize you publicly in front of everyone, with your shame on display to all of your colleagues, who will then perceive this failure as a possible persistent pattern.

Bonus Rewards: Regardless of A or B, you angered your colleagues, didn't discuss your presentation idea with the group before meeting with the boss, and displayed "anti-grouped" behavior.

In Japan, the concept of harmony and avoiding conflict are highly valued. Therefore, standing out too much or being too outspoken can be perceived as aggressive or arrogant, even if that is not your intention. By understanding the proverb "The tallest nail is hammered first," you can better understand how Japanese people perceive those who stand out too much and work to avoid making these mistakes yourself.

However, it is essential to note that this does not mean you should completely suppress your individuality. Balancing fitting into the group and expressing your unique qualities is vital. By finding ways to contribute to the group while still being true to yourself, you can demonstrate your value as a team member while respecting Japanese cultural norms.

Another reason why understanding this proverb is crucial for foreigners working in Japan is that it highlights the importance of humility and modesty. In a collectivistic society, individuals are expected to downplay their accomplishments and not draw too much attention to themselves. Japanese collectivism can be challenging for people from different cultures, where self-promotion and assertiveness are often encouraged.

It is essential to cultivate a humble and modest attitude rather than boasting about your accomplishments. Try focusing on contributing to the team and helping others succeed. By respecting the group and prioritizing the common good, you can demonstrate your commitment to the company's success and build meaningful relationships with your Japanese colleagues.

Understanding the proverb "The tallest nail is hammered first" is essential for anyone looking to work in Japan. By recognizing the importance of group harmony and avoiding standing out too much, you can demonstrate your respect for Japanese cultural norms and build meaningful relationships with your colleagues. By cultivating a humble and modest attitude, you can show your commitment to the team's success while expressing your unique qualities.

Chapter Six: The Unrelenting Fear of Failure

In Japan's modern work culture, the fear of failure is deeply ingrained in the mindset of many Japanese employees. This fear stems from a cultural emphasis on perfectionism, conformity, and group harmony. Failure is often seen as a source of shame and a threat to the reputation of individuals and teams.

Understanding the roots of this fear is crucial for any foreigner seeking to work in Japan. While it may seem counterintuitive, recognizing the role of failure in personal and professional growth can improve a team's productivity and success.

One key factor contributing to the fear of failure is the Japanese education system, which places a high value on rote memorization and the ability to pass exams. This emphasis on getting the correct answer can create a mentality that mistakes are unacceptable and can lead to a reluctance to take risks.

Moreover, Japan's strong emphasis on group harmony also plays a role in the aversion to failure. In many workplaces, the team is viewed as a single entity, and the success or failure of one individual reflects on the entire group. Fear of failure creates a culture where employees are more concerned about maintaining the group's reputation than their own. It is essential to understand that failure is not necessarily a reflection of personal incompetence or weakness; it can be an opportunity to learn and improve. Adopting a growth mindset that focuses on learning from mistakes and embracing challenges can help overcome the fear of failure and ultimately lead to tremendous success.

One way to address failure in the Japanese workplace is to create a psychological safety culture. A safety culture means fostering an environment where employees feel comfortable taking risks and sharing their ideas without fear of retribution or ridicule. Encouraging open communication and constructive feedback can help create a sense of trust and teamwork that enables employees to take calculated risks and learn from their failures.

In addition, reframing failure as a necessary step toward success can help shift attitudes and reduce the stigma associated with mistakes. Reducing stigma involves recognizing the potential for failure in any endeavor and being prepared to learn from it when it occurs. Viewing failure as a learning opportunity can help foster resilience and adaptability, which are essential for success in any field.

Don't worry about minor things like "forgetting to type the page numbers at the bottom of a page" or "I got an ink stain on my shirt," but you will notice that when it comes to more important things, your colleagues and superiors will seem ruthless. Every group member has a task that makes the group function. Therefore, in their minds, you are not doing your portion. You are forcing everyone else to work harder. You are being selfish and not thinking about the group. If you are not completing your specific task, it is viewed as a dereliction of duty against the group. The group is utterly content with discarding a malfunctioning part instead of trying to fix it, even if it is simple. If you are the "root" cause of failure within the group, you take all the blame in one go.

A good analogy would be to think of failure like a vial of poison, but only enough for one person. If one person is to blame, they must drink the entire vial ending their life. But if it is a group failure, eight people must share an equal portion of the vial. Drinking the poison as a group would mean the group would survive, but there may be non-terminal side effects. So, if you fail alone, you will know almost immediately. Failure in Japan also applies to things that are out of your control with something like:

The train is late, and you were 15min late for an important meeting.
Your child woke up feeling sick, and you needed to take them to the doctor while a project deadline was due.

The excuse doesn't matter. Whether or not you are doing your portion for the group is what the group cares about.

While Japan's cultural emphasis on perfectionism and group harmony can create a fear of failure in the workplace, it is crucial to recognize the role of failure in personal and professional growth. Adopting a growth mindset and creating a culture of psychological safety can overcome this fear and create a workplace culture that values learning, innovation, and success.

PART II: Getting to Know the Hierarchy System of Your Company

Chapter Seven: Navigating the Japanese Hierarchy of Your Company

In Japanese culture, hierarchy is crucial to social and professional life. Understanding this hierarchy is essential for anyone looking to work in Japan and build successful relationships with Japanese colleagues. In this article, we will explore the Japanese hierarchy and provide tips on how to navigate it effectively.

The Japanese hierarchy is deeply ingrained in society based on age, status, and seniority. It is a system where those in higher positions are respected and revered, and those in lower positions are expected to show deference and obedience. This hierarchy is present in all aspects of Japanese life, from the family to the workplace.

In the workplace, the hierarchy is fundamental, and it is essential to understand the various levels and their corresponding roles. The most senior position in a Japanese company is the president or CEO, followed by the vice presidents, managers, and regular employees. Within each level, further divisions may be based on seniority and experience.

As a foreigner working in Japan, it is essential to understand the hierarchy and the expectations around it. Showing respect for those in higher positions is crucial, and you should always address them with the appropriate honorifics. For example, using "san" after someone's name shows respect, while using "sama" offers even more respect.

Additionally, being mindful of your behavior and language when interacting with those in higher positions is essential. Speaking too loudly or being too informal can be viewed as disrespectful, so it is critical to err on the side of caution and follow the lead of your Japanese colleagues.

Another critical aspect of the Japanese hierarchy is the concept of "senpai" and "kohai." In Japanese culture, seniority is highly respected, and those who have been with the company longer are expected to mentor and guide those who are newer or less experienced. This relationship is known as "senpai-kohai," and it is an essential part of Japanese culture.

As a foreigner working in Japan, it is essential to understand the senpai-kohai relationship and show respect for more senior people. It is also crucial to be willing to learn from your senpai and seek guidance when needed. By demonstrating a willingness to learn and a respect for seniority, you can build strong relationships with your colleagues and succeed in the workplace.

Finally, it is essential to understand that the Japanese hierarchy extends beyond the workplace and into all aspects of life. For example, age is highly respected in Japan, and showing respect for those older than you is essential. Additionally, the concept of "uchi-soto" (inside-outside) is necessary for Japanese culture, and it refers to the distinction between those who are part of the group (uchi) and those who are not (soto).

As a foreigner working in Japan, it is essential to understand the uchi-soto dynamic and work to become part of the group. Uchi-Soto may take time and effort, but you can become a valued team member by respecting Japanese culture, being mindful of your behavior and language, and building solid relationships with your colleagues.

Japanese hierarchy is essential for anyone looking to work in Japan. By respecting those in higher positions, understanding the senpai-kohai relationship, and being mindful of the uchi-soto dynamic, you can build strong relationships with your Japanese colleagues and succeed in the workplace. With these principles in mind, you can confidently navigate the Japanese hierarchy and succeed in your career.

Chapter Eight: What is Sempai?...No Seriously?

If you're planning to work in Japan, you may come across the term "sempai" quite frequently. It is a Japanese word that refers to someone senior to you, usually in actual age or time spent with the company. Sempai is an essential concept in Japanese culture, particularly in the workplace, where it plays a vital role in establishing and maintaining relationships between colleagues.

Appreciating the Japanese emphasis on hierarchy and respect for authority is essential. In Japan, social status and rank are highly valued, and individuals are expected to defer to those senior to them in age, experience, or position. A strict hierarchy is particularly evident in the workplace, where the Japanese approach to management emphasizes the importance of harmony and cooperation within a team.

In this context, sempai refers to someone more experienced than you in a particular field or who has worked in the company longer than you. It is a term of respect and acknowledgment, implying that the person has valuable knowledge and skills to be learned and passed on. As such, you must show deference to your sempai and seek their guidance and support as you navigate the workplace. The oldest sempai has seniority over the group and tends to be the person that makes decisions. This position is not something you won over with merit. You have to "wait your turn."

Sometimes, a sempai may "abdicate" their formal leadership position with the prospect of doing less work, letting the "next in line" take the mantle. However, that next leader will confer everything with the abdicated leader because they are still "sempai." So the original "head sempai" becomes a "shadow sempai." Shadow sempai often happens, especially when a "head sempai" is close to retirement.

However, sempai is not just a one-way relationship but a matter of junior employees deferring to their seniors. The relationship between sempai and kohai is reciprocal, with the sempai taking on a mentorship role and providing guidance and support to their kohai. In contrast, the kohai shows respect and loyalty to their sempai.

This respect is reflected in the Japanese concept of "senpai-kohai culture," which emphasizes the importance of these relationships in building a solid and cohesive team. In this culture, the sempai is expected to take an active interest in the development and well-being of their kohai and offer guidance and support as needed. Kohai are expected to show loyalty and respect to their sempai. They should also be willing to learn from sempai's experience and knowledge.

As a foreigner working in Japan, understanding the importance of sempai relationships is essential for building meaningful relationships with your colleagues and succeeding in the workplace. By showing respect for your sempai, seeking their guidance and support, and being open to learning from their experience, you can demonstrate your commitment to the team and build a strong network of support and mentorship.

However, it is also important to remember that sempai relationships are not hierarchical or rigidly defined. Instead, they are fluid and dynamic, with different people taking on the role of sempai or kohai, depending on the context and the situation. As such, it is essential to be flexible and adaptable in your approach to these relationships. Your colleagues and bosses will praise your willingness to learn from and collaborate with people at all levels of the organization significantly.

There is a balance to the system when you have seniority where if you try to delegate all your work to someone else, your sempai will notice and reverse it. But there is usually an "acceptable" amount of unequal distribution of tasks depending on seniority regardless. One of the downsides to being kohai is that you are typically given jobs the superiors don't want to do. One of the upsides is that when it comes to parties or dinners, in Japan, you always split the bill in a group. Sempai pays more towards the total bill depending on how high their sempai status is. So, you are drinking on Sempai's dime. This method of paying is viewed as socially obligatory in a group setting.

However, if you are "greedy" or "scornful," you may get invited to a private lunch with sempai, and they'll ask you to pay in retaliation. This system has existed since Japan began, and there is no way to get around it. It will seem unfair, but you get more perks as time progresses. Because this system was imposed on the "head sempai" when they were a kohai, it is viewed as a "birthright" to continue the sempai/kohai relationship.

Ultimately, sempai is about building strong and supportive relationships within the workplace and fostering a culture of respect, mentorship, and collaboration. By embracing this culture and seeking to develop meaningful relationships with your colleagues, you can succeed in the Japanese workplace and contribute to the growth and success of your team.

Chapter Nine: How Decisions Are Made in a Japanese Company

In Japan, decision-making is often a collaborative process involving input from multiple organizational levels. Multi-level collaboration can sometimes make the decision-making process slower and more deliberate than in other countries. Still, it also means that decisions are often well-considered and based on a consensus of the group.

One important concept to understand is "nemawashi" (digging around the roots), which refers to laying the groundwork for a decision by seeking input and building consensus among stakeholders before making an official decision. Nemawashi often involves multiple meetings and discussions among departments and individuals to ensure everyone's opinions and concerns are heard and addressed.

Another critical aspect of decision-making in Japan is the principle of "ringi," which refers to circulating a document or proposal to relevant parties within the organization for review and approval. This process can be formal, with each individual adding their seal or stamp to the document as a sign of support. This process aims to ensure that everyone involved in the decision-making process has a chance to review and comment on the proposal before it is finalized.

In Japanese companies, decisions are often made by senior managers or executives, who have the final say on important matters. However, even in hierarchical organizations, it's essential to understand that decisions are often made through a consensus-building process involving input from multiple organizational levels. Familiarizing yourself with the decision-making process means building relationships and seeking information from colleagues and superiors at all levels of the organization to ensure that your opinions and concerns are heard and considered.

One way to navigate the decision-making process in Japan as a foreigner is to focus on building solid relationships with colleagues and superiors. Making the necessary relationships involves respecting Japanese culture and customs and demonstrating a willingness to listen and learn from others. It's also important to be patient and persistent in seeking input and building consensus, as the decision-making process in Japan can sometimes be slower than in other countries.

Another essential strategy is to seek a mentor or "senpai" within the organization who can guide and support you as you navigate the decision-making process. This person can help you understand the organization's culture and values and provide insights into how decisions are made and who the key players are. Likely, to speak to or ask something the Boss, you'll have to:

1. Talk with the Highest Sempai in your group. If yes, then move to 2. If they say no, you can't.
2. Then they talk with the Group Leader. If yes, then move to 3. If they say no, you can't.
3. Then they talk with the Group Manager. If yes, then move to 4. If they say no, you can't.
4. Then they talk with the Department Secretary. If yes, then move to 5. If they say no, you can't.
5.   Then they talk with the Department Manager. If yes, then move to 6. If they say no, you can't.
6. Then they talk with the Boss.

Skipping steps will be anti-collective as these superiors must be spoken to individually and will make the person you ask question your group priority.

The person you skipped will think you are trying to circumvent their position. It might seem reductive but powerful positions in Japan come with many risks. Even something as simple as changing the kind of paper you use could impact a superior's work or pride. The likelihood of someone on the base level saying "No" is very high. You may find your boss saying "No" abruptly, then one month later, implement your idea word for word under the assumption that it was the boss' idea. Constant and consistent rejection is standard, don't fight it. Almost always, "no" is how the system works, which happened to your boss when he was initially in your position. The status quo and the rejection of new ideas and policies are how Japan has done things since the dawn of Japan; they will not change.

The decision-making process in a Japanese company is a crucial aspect of being an influential team member. By understanding the principles of "nemawashi" and "ringi," as well as the importance of relationships and consensus-building, you can contribute to the organization's success and build meaningful relationships with your colleagues and superiors. By seeking a mentor and demonstrating a willingness to learn and adapt to Japanese culture and customs, you can confidently navigate the decision-making process and contribute to the company's long-term success.

Chapter Ten: Where Am I in All of This?

Entering a new job in a foreign country can be a daunting experience, especially when you're in an entry-level position at a company. Japan, with its unique culture and customs, can add an extra layer of complexity to the experience. But fear not. With the right mindset and preparation, your entry-level position can be a valuable learning experience and the start of a fulfilling career in Japan.

It's important to remember that your role in the company is also important, no matter how small it may seem. The Japanese term for this is "ichi-nichi-issho," which means "one day, one life." It reminds us that every day is precious and every task can contribute to the company's success, no matter how seemingly insignificant. This perspective lets you approach your entry-level position purposefully and strive to do your best.

Another aspect of being in an entry-level position in Japan is the focus on training and learning. In many Japanese companies, new employees undergo intensive training and onboarding to learn the company's policies and procedures and the skills required for their job. These skills can include technical and soft skills such as communication and teamwork.

While this can be overwhelming sometimes, it's important to remember that the company is investing in your development as a professional. Take advantage of the training opportunities provided and be open to learning from your colleagues and superiors. If you need clarification, feel free to ask questions or seek guidance from your sempai.

At the same time, it's crucial to maintain a positive attitude and approach your work with enthusiasm. Maintaining enthusiasm can help you build relationships with your colleagues and superiors, which can be critical in a hierarchical work environment like Japan. By showing a willingness to learn and contribute, you can demonstrate your commitment to the company and set yourself up for success in the future.

One potential challenge of being in an entry-level position in Japan is the focus on seniority and tenure. In many Japanese companies, promotions and career advancement are often tied to a length of service and seniority. A seniority-based system can frustrate foreign employees who may be accustomed to a more merit-based system.

However, it's important to remember that this system is deeply ingrained in Japanese culture rather than something that can be easily changed. Instead, focus on building your skills and experience, and look for meaningful opportunities to contribute to the company. Over time, your hard work and dedication are recognized and rewarded.

Knowing when and how to be helpful to someone in a position of authority is very important. Remember, your opinion matters little to the people at the top. Furthermore, you would not give your ideas freely in groupthink because it would separate you from the group. There are some unconventional ways around it, in any case. Just because your opinion doesn't matter doesn't mean you are ignored—just the opposite. Most superiors are well aware of your duties and behaviors. Instead of stating your opinion directly, you should reframe the end goal so the boss gets the credit.

For example, you know one kind of paper would be best for the company, but if you tell the boss, "We should change to brand 'A' because of 'X' reason," you'll be rejected outright. Your opinion challenges the authority and pride of your boss, who ultimately makes decisions. It is not groupthink and would alienate you from your group, and it could lead to some dangerous assumptions. But if you were to print out two copies on separate paper, ask the boss, "Which one do you think looks best for our company?" and the boss says he likes the new brand. Then you tell him our office currently uses brand 'B' and ask if that will be ok. It puts the boss in the decision-making position and removes your opinion from the ordeal. You intended to change the paper, but your opinion remained hidden, and your boss claimed the credit. You are off the hook within the group when the boss changes the paper.

Remember to take care of yourself and maintain a healthy work-life balance. In Japan, there is a strong emphasis on working hard and long hours, which can be challenging for foreigners who may need to become more accustomed to this lifestyle. However, it's crucial to prioritize your health and well-being to perform your best at work.

Maintaining your well-being can include taking breaks throughout the day, getting enough sleep and exercise, and maintaining a social support network outside of work. Taking care of yourself will better equip you to handle the challenges and opportunities of being in an entry-level position in Japan.

Being in an entry-level position in Japan can be a challenging but rewarding experience. By adapting to the culture, approaching your work with purpose and enthusiasm, and focusing on learning and growth, you can build a solid foundation for a successful career in Japan. Remember to be patient, persistent, and proactive in your approach to work, and don't be afraid to ask for help or guidance when needed. With the right mindset and attitude, you can make the most of your entry-level position and set yourself up for long-term success in the Japanese workplace.

PART III: Company Norms Throughout Most Sectors

Chapter Eleven: How Contracts Look and Work

Your contract type can determine many aspects of your employment, including salary, working hours, benefits, and job security. This article will discuss the main types of contracts you may encounter in Japan and what you need to know about them.

One of Japan's most common types of contracts is the "shain" (正社員) contract. This permanent full-time contract offers job security and benefits such as health insurance, pension contributions, and paid vacation. In many Japanese companies, becoming a "shain" employee signifies success and stability, and it's a highly coveted position that offers stability and the potential for career advancement.

Getting a "shain" contract is not always easy, especially for foreigners who may be new to the country or the company. Many Japanese companies have strict requirements for becoming a "shain" employee, such as passing a probationary period or meeting specific performance standards. It's important to clarify these requirements with your employer early on in your employment to ensure understanding and satisfaction later.

Another type of contract in Japan is the "haken" (派遣) contract, a temporary worker contract. This type of contract is typically offered by staffing agencies that provide workers to companies temporarily. As a "haken" worker, you may have less job security and fewer benefits than a "shain" employee. Still, you may also have more flexibility and the opportunity to work in various industries and roles.

One advantage of a "haken" contract is that it can be a way to get your foot in the door with a company and gain valuable experience. Many "haken" workers become "shain" employees or secure other permanent positions based on their performance and work ethic. However, it's essential to know that "haken" contracts can also come with certain risks, such as sudden termination or lack of job stability.

A third type of contract you may encounter in Japan is the "keiyaku-shain" (契約社員) contract, also known as a fixed-term contract. This type of contract is similar to a "shain" contract regarding benefits and job duties but has a set expiration date. "Keiyaku-shain" contracts are often used to cover temporary staff shortages or to provide a trial period before offering a permanent position.

If you're offered a "keiyaku-shain" contract, it's essential to understand the contract terms and the reasons for the fixed-term duration. Some employers may renew "keiyaku-shain" contracts multiple times, while others may use them to avoid providing permanent employment status. Be sure to clarify your career prospects and potential for advancement with your employer if you're considering a "keiyaku-shain" contract. In the past, Japan had a rule that if you contract under a "keiyaku-shain" for five years consecutively, the company should hire you as "shain" during the 6th year.

In addition to these main types of contracts, there are also various other types of non-permanent agreements, such as "arubaito" (part-time) contracts and "gyomu-itaku" (business outsourcing) contracts. These contracts typically offer fewer benefits and less job security than "shain" or "keiyaku-shain" contracts. Still, they may provide more flexibility and variety regarding work hours and job duties.

In Japan, the accounting year runs from April 1st to March 31st of the following year, and many companies and organizations operate on this cycle. "Kaikeinendo" employees are hired temporarily during a specific accounting year and are typically employed to cover temporary staff shortages or work on short-term projects. This contract outlines the terms and conditions of employment for accounting year employees. It typically includes details such as the duration of employment, salary, working hours, job duties, and any benefits or allowances to which the employee is entitled.

The contract for accounting year employees is similar to the "keiyaku-shain" (fixed-term) contract in that it has a set expiration date and offers fewer benefits and less job security than a permanent "shain" contract. However, it may be a good option for individuals looking for short-term employment opportunities or wanting to gain experience in a specific industry or role. This contracting style was added in 2020 as a workaround to the 5-year "keiyaku-shain" rule in favor of perpetual yearly contracting. Note that the company can remove the position at the end of the contract period.

When considering different types of contracts in Japan, weighing each option's benefits and drawbacks and considering your career goals and priorities is essential. Suppose job security and stability are important to you. In that case, a "shain" or "keiyaku-shain" contract may be the best fit, while if you're looking for more flexibility and variety in your work, a temporary or part-time contract may be a better option. It's also essential to research the company and industry you're interested in and understand their hiring practices and requirements.

If you're a foreigner looking to work in Japan, you must know the cultural and language differences that may impact your employment prospects. Building relationships and networking with Japanese colleagues and employers can be crucial in securing a job and advancing your career in Japan.

It's essential to understand and abide by Japanese labor laws and regulations, which can differ from those in your home country. For example, Japanese labor laws dictate maximum working hours, overtime pay, and mandatory insurance contributions. Failing to comply with these laws can result in legal and financial consequences.

Japan's different contracts are essential for anyone looking to work there. Each type of contract has its benefits and drawbacks, and it's necessary to consider your career goals and priorities when choosing a contract. Building relationships with Japanese colleagues and understanding Japanese labor laws can also be crucial to success in the Japanese workplace.

Chapter Twelve: How Full-Time and Part-Time Work Differ

Many aspects of contracts require companies to give specific benefits, whether someone is full-time or part-time. A key factor to remember is that 30 hours or more is considered "Full-Time." Full-time employment comes with benefits like 20 days a year of vacation/sick leave (specific industries have exceptions like the medical industry), Shakai Hoken (company health insurance stipend), and Kousei Nenkin (company pension stipend). Also, you get a slew of paid days off for hospitalization, hospice care, death in the family, and particular holiday time off.

These are all great, but they are not present for "Part-time" employees. Part-time employees get ten days a year of vacation/sick leave and no other things that reduce their overall expenditures (the stipends) for the month. Knowing what part-time means in Japan is vital as companies looking to hire people abroad will advertise 29.5 hours a week and 250,000 yen a month (250,000 yen spends like $2500 even though the currency goes up and down). These companies may be your only option to get a visa to Japan initially. Part-time does have its freedom, especially if you are not carrying around much debt when you get to Japan. If you have debt, you may spend more time saving and doing less travel to compensate for your financial needs.

(This next section is of the full-time and part-time section for ALTs "Assistant Language Teachers" and will discuss the "gyomu-itaku" process as it pertains to entry-level teaching jobs in Japan. If this doesn't interest you, please skip to the next section)

Japan has a series of companies that source ALTs for different schools. These companies are called "gyomu-itaku-kaisha." They are not a teaching organization but contract teachers annually or annually. Usually, your contract periods are either April 1st to March 31st or August (pending) to March 31st.

During this time, the company acts as a middleman between you and the school and will tell you your duties. Because they are a dispatch company, you can only change your schedule with their approval. Likewise, it is the same for any teacher you work with. These duties vary policy can be a hassle for you or your JTE "Japanese Teacher of English." It is best to use this process only when necessary, like a double booking or a complete schedule change.

Every, and I do mean every, "gyomu-itaku kaisha" that caters to education has all of their employees under a 29.5hours per week contract. They do this, so they are not required to grant Full-Time benefits. Your agreement says that you must work 8 am-5 pm every day, and if you add up the hours, You may be saying, "Hey, isn't that 45hrs a week?" Unfortunately, your contract only calculates the hours spent teaching in a classroom during a teaching period. Japan has six periods plus lunch, and the max time spent in each class is 50min. So if you calculate five days times seven periods, you get 35. Now times 35 by 50min, and you get 29.16 hours a week. Because they only calculate your classroom hours, you aren't paid before your first class from 8 am to 8:45 am and not from 3 pm to 5 pm. Remember that you are contractually obligated to be at the school during those times.

These "gyomu-itaku kaisha" have a high turnover rate, and most employees try to leave within the first year or two. Because of this, few people are challenging the system in place. Those that have are black-listed from working for these companies. This employment problem is also a "foreigner's" issue, which means it is not necessarily a concern to the Japanese public. If you must work for one of these companies, looking for other employment immediately after getting your visa is highly recommended. It is advised to be ready to change jobs at the end of your contracted period. Remember that while you can shift employment mid-contract, it is highly recommended against it as you may have issues finding employment with other companies offering the same or similar services.

If a company that employed Japanese people were to try and use the same labor practices, they would be branded a "buraku kaisha" meaning Black Company. A Black Company tries to get labor out of its employees by removing the cultural benefits from standard contracts and forcing employees through collective coercion to overperform beyond the legal requirements. The public is well aware that these companies exist and will passively boycott them if they offer services to them. Regarding teaching, the parents don't see the dispatch companies as a service; neither do the teachers. The company is hired through the Board of Education in the city. Because there is this abstraction layer, Japanese people tend to ignore it or are completely oblivious to it. Be sure to research the company you plan to work for and see the comments from former and current employees.

Chapter Thirteen: Describing Your Day-to-Day Work Life

Three things in life are always consistent death, taxes, and Japanese train schedules. If you are on a central line in Tokyo or Osaka with a one-minute delay, you can get an excuse card with a written apology from the train company to take to work as your excuse for being late. And it is generally an accepted thing because it is scarce. But let's talk about your daily life using your contractually stated 9 am-5 pm job. Here is your day as a new hire for a Japanese company.

(Your day starts with how long it takes you to prepare to leave at 7:30 am. Your commute to work is 30min via walking and train. You arrive at work at 8 am. It is you and another person that just started working at the company. You begin your duties checking to ensure the trash is taken care of and the toilets are clean. As people arrive, you greet them with a more profound bow and "Ohayo gozaimasu." Some of the other people around your status begin to help with the general cleaning. Mid to high-tier sempai sit at their desks and prepare. At 9 am, a building-wide chime sounds, and you clock in for work. And you work, with another chime at noon, taking an hour break at lunch. It is dead silent, and no one talks with anyone. You notice three or four people go to the tatami room with pillows. They return at 1:00 pm as the second chime starts, and people begin working again. At 3:30 pm, you and the other person from the morning make tea and set out snacks making sure the boss' room is tidy. At 4 pm, guests arrive to meet the boss. At 5 pm, there is another building-wide chime, you clock out of work, and everyone remains at their desk continuing to work. The boss is in a meeting, and it has gone over time. At 7 pm, the guests leave the boss' office. You and the other worker clean up after the guests. The boss exits the building before you finish and do the other employees shortly after. It is 8 pm, and you get your things and go home. You are paid from 9 am to 5 pm.)

Now, this seems unsettling, and to an extent, it is. But this is a very ordinary day in Japan. Certain social norms related to Japanese work culture go beyond the confines of your contractual obligations. Remember when we talked about Perception? I purposefully told everything before this to set up the example scenario you read. Now after explaining the different levels of hierarchy, perception, collectivism, and social power, you can probably see where I will go next in my explanations as to why a person's daily Japanese life is like this.

(Before you read on, consider why a person wouldn't just clock in and out from 9 am-5 pm.)

The person coming to work at 8 am is trying to give off the perception that they are loyal to the company, not by "working overtime" but by being attentive to the company's daily needs. Many private companies in Japan either have minimal or do not hire cleaning staff, and the employees usually do that. The kohai is expected to take on the task of cleaning and preparation for the company. Older members are given a break and can come in closer to 9 am because they have proven loyal to the company in previous years.

Lunch is exciting in Japan. There is usually a tatami room (Japanese guest room with Japanese mats), and people will finish their lunch in less than ten minutes and nap there. It is common for four or five people to share the same room. Usually, all the lights go off in the office at lunch to conserve electricity, and people will take out their phones to do searches. No one uses their cell phone during work hours, and lunch is unplugged time.

You don't talk with anyone. This unspoken agreement between colleagues is that they don't have to interact with anyone during lunch. Don't talk with anyone unprompted. And if someone approaches you to talk about something non-work related, you can assume it is genuine because it is rare.

Like before, when it comes to guests, you are in charge of cleaning. If you are a woman, it will be expected of you to make tea. No one will tell you; they will assume you know to do it and to serve it. I know it seems sexist, and it is, but that is the expectation. If you are younger, you have more of an obligation. Same with clean up. I don't think men are off the hook. If there are no more youthful women and older women in higher positions, they may make younger men serve the tea. Most of these duties will be explained to you when you first arrive.

Lastly, no one leaves until the boss leaves. Once the boss exits the building, people go out slowly. Sometimes the boss leaves right at 5 pm. Sometimes he's on a business trip, and you can leave at 5 pm. But if you leave before he does and aren't taking paid/unpaid time off, people's perceptions of you will degrade.

Chapter Fourteen: I Heard That Japanese People are Workaholics. Is That True?

Japan's postwar period was a time of rapid economic growth and transformation, fueled by a strong work ethic that defined the country's national identity. The work culture of many Japanese workers during this time was not simply the result of cultural or personal preference but rather a product of various historical, social, and economic factors that shaped Japan's postwar society.

One major factor that contributed to Japan's work culture was the country's experience of postwar reconstruction. In the aftermath of World War II, Japan faced immense challenges in rebuilding its infrastructure, industries, and economy. The Japanese government and business leaders recognized the urgent need for rapid industrialization and economic growth to restore the country's status as a significant global power.

Japan adopted an industrial development model emphasizing productivity, efficiency, and hard work to achieve this goal. The government and business leaders promoted a culture of dedication, sacrifice, and discipline necessary for national success and individual advancement. This ideology became known as the "Japanese work ethic" or "salaryman culture," and it shaped the values and expectations of generations of Japanese workers.

Another factor contributing to Japan's work culture was the social and economic changes that occurred in the postwar period. As Japan's economy grew and diversified, new industries and job opportunities emerged, particularly in technology, manufacturing, and finance. The competition for skilled and talented workers was fierce, and many companies sought to attract and retain employees through high salaries, benefits, and job security.

However, in exchange for these rewards, many Japanese workers were expected to work long hours, often far beyond the standard 40-hour workweek. The norm in many Japanese companies was for employees to work 12 hours a day or more, with only a few days off each month. This grueling schedule was often seen as a mark of dedication and loyalty to the company. Workers who failed to meet these expectations risked being seen as lazy or uncommitted.

A third factor contributing to Japan's work culture was the role of the family and social networks in Japanese society. In traditional Japanese culture, the family and community were highly valued and played a central role in shaping individual identity and behavior. This emphasis on social connection and obligation carried over into the workplace, where companies often functioned as extended families or social networks.

Many Japanese workers viewed their job as more than just a means of making a living; it was also a source of social identity and belonging. The strong bonds between coworkers and the sense of shared purpose and responsibility often led to a willingness to work long hours and sacrifice personal time for the group's good. This obligation to the company and the community contributes to the prevalence of unpaid overtime work. Shared purpose makes workers reluctant to take a vacation or sick leave.

Japan's postwar work culture was a complex phenomenon that emerged from a combination of historical, social, and economic factors. The country's experience of postwar reconstruction, the competition for skilled labor, and the role of family and community in Japanese society all shaped the values and expectations of Japanese workers. While this work ethic has been celebrated for its contributions to Japan's economic success, it has also been criticized for its toll on worker health, family life, and overall quality of life. As a foreigner considering working in Japan, knowing these cultural and historical factors and weighing the benefits and drawbacks of Japan's work culture for your personal and professional goals is essential.

While the sempai system can be valuable in professional development, it can also contribute to a workaholic culture. One reason is that senpai often feels a sense of responsibility for a kouhai's success, which can translate into working longer hours and taking on more responsibilities. This feeling of mentorship is especially true in industries like finance and law, where long hours are the norm and competition for promotions is fierce. Senpai may feel they must set an example for their kohai and show them the dedication and work ethic required to succeed in the industry.

The "Wa" can lead to a situation where people feel pressure to work longer hours to avoid inconveniencing or burdening their colleagues. Sometimes, this can become a form of one-upmanship, where people compete to see who can perform the most prolonged hours or take on the most difficult tasks.

Another factor contributing to Japan's workaholic culture is the importance of seniority in the workplace. In many Japanese companies, promotions and pay raises are based on years of service rather than merit or performance. This seniority system means that younger employees may feel they must work long hours and demonstrate their dedication to be considered for future promotions. A need to prove your abilities can create a cycle where employees feel pressure to work longer hours to get ahead, even if it is not necessary for their job responsibilities.

The cultural expectation of "ganbaru," or do your best, in Japan can manifest as a sense of obligation to work long hours and put in extra effort, even if it is not required. This cultural expectation is often reinforced by family, social pressure, and media portrayals of successful individuals who have achieved their goals through hard work and perseverance.

Not all Japanese people participate in this workaholic culture, and there are growing efforts to address the issue. Some companies are implementing policies to reduce working hours, such as limiting overtime or promoting work-life balance. The Japanese government has also introduced legislation to reduce the prevalence of overwork and promote healthier work environments.

It is essential to be aware of these cultural expectations and to find a balance that works for you. While it can be valuable to demonstrate dedication and a strong work ethic, it is also essential to prioritize your physical and mental health. It is okay to set boundaries and to communicate your needs with your colleagues and superiors. By finding a balance that works for you, you can succeed in your career without sacrificing your well-being.

Chapter Fifteen: Working in a Group in the Collective

Teamwork and collaboration are deeply ingrained in Japanese society, reflected in how businesses operate. As a foreigner working in Japan, it's crucial to understand how group projects work and how you can contribute to their success.

In Japanese companies, group projects are often organized around "nemawashi," which means "laying the groundwork." Nemawashi involves extensive communication and collaboration among team members to ensure everyone is on the same page and that decisions are made by consensus. Meetings are often held to discuss the project, and all team members are encouraged to share their opinions and ideas.

One important aspect of group projects in Japan is the role of the company president, or "shacho." They are responsible for setting the project's direction and ensuring everyone works together effectively. They also play an essential role in maintaining group harmony and addressing conflicts.

Respect for seniority is an essential aspect of Japanese culture, reflected in how group projects are organized. Junior members are expected to defer to senior members' opinions and show respect for their experience and knowledge, even if they are making a grave mistake. "Waiting Your Turn" is the mantra of the Japanese company worker.

Communication is also crucial in Japanese group projects. Team members are expected to communicate openly and honestly with each other and to be receptive to feedback and criticism. This kind of receptiveness can be challenging for foreigners from cultures that value individualism and personal achievement more. However, it's important to remember that in Japan, the group's success is often more important than the success of any one individual.

In addition to communication, attention to detail is critical in Japanese group projects. Japanese companies place a high value on quality and precision, reflected in how projects are executed. Team members are expected to pay close attention to every project aspect and strive for perfection in everything they do.

As a foreigner working on a group project in Japan, it's essential to be aware of these cultural norms and to adjust your behavior accordingly. Work cultural norms may mean being more submissive to senior members or more conscious of the need for consensus-building and open communication. It's also important to be patient and persistent, as group projects in Japan often take longer than they would in other cultures.

So how does your typical Japanese group project operate? Here is a good idea of what to expect working on a Japanese group project:

In a group of six plus one group leader, two will do most of the work, and three will do almost nothing. One was there at the initial meeting but needs to contribute more and is oblivious to any changes, ideas, or advice. But they are added because they were at the initial meeting, and blame for a failure can be more easily spread between seven people rather than two. The project was for three months. On the last day, three hours before the deadline, the group leader, that was not a part of any meetings or work but had been watching the project like a hawk, pokes his head into the room and asks, "Can I help you guys with the deadline?". The group knows that the project has some basic formatting checks needed, and because sempai is asking, they are required to say "yes." Sempai then finishes the 45min worth of formatting, slaps their name on the very top of the project, and puts the rest of the team in the mentions in the back. They then submit the assignment. The group leader gets the majority of the recognition from the superiors. Then if the group goes out for drinks to celebrate the project's completion, no one talks about the project at the party. And when the people doing most of the work start becoming group leaders, they are expected to do the same that their group leaders did to them. Japan does this and has done things since the dawn of Japan. It will not change.

Group projects are essential to Japan's modern work culture, and understanding how they work is critical for success in a Japanese workplace. By being mindful of cultural norms and adapting your behavior accordingly, you can contribute to the group's success and build strong relationships with your colleagues.

PART IV: Japanese Cultural Norms to Know Before You Start

Chapter Sixteen: Punctuality and Keeping Time

Punctuality is highly valued in Japan's modern work culture and is often seen as a reflection of an individual's work ethic and professionalism. It is considered rude and disrespectful to arrive late to a meeting or appointment in Japan. For a foreigner who wants to work in Japan, punctuality is essential to thriving in the workplace.

Being on time shows respect for other people's time, showing that you value their opinions and contributions. Arriving early to a meeting or appointment in Japan is even better, as it allows you to prepare yourself and demonstrate your eagerness and commitment. In Japanese culture, waiting outside the meeting room until the appointed time is typical as a sign of respect for the person hosting the meeting.

Punctuality is essential not only for meetings and appointments but also for daily work routines. Japanese companies have strict start and end times, and employees are expected to arrive on time and leave only after finishing all their daily tasks. Being punctual also helps ensure that work processes run smoothly, as delays can cause disruptions and affect productivity.

Another aspect of punctuality in Japan is the concept of "jikan no mottainai," which means "not wasting time." In Japan, time is a valuable resource you should use wisely. Punctuality is one way to show you are making the most of it. For example, if a meeting is scheduled for an hour, all agenda items will be covered within that time frame. Everyone at the conference will be ready to move on to their next task after the meeting.

Punctuality is seen as a sign of respect and professionalism in Japan. Punctuality is also seen as maintaining harmony and order in the workplace. By arriving on time, everyone can start and end their workday with less workflow disruption. Keeping your schedule in order creates a sense of unity and shared purpose, which is highly valued in Japanese culture.

Overall, understanding the importance of punctuality in Japan's modern work culture is essential for anyone who wants to work in Japan. Being on time shows respect for others, helps ensure smooth work processes and promotes harmony and order in the workplace. So, if you want to succeed in a Japanese work environment, always arrive on time, or even better, a few minutes early.

Chapter Seventeen: Gift-Giving Practices

In Japan's modern work culture, gift-giving after a business trip or vacation is a courteous gesture essential to building and maintaining business relationships. If you're a foreigner who wants to work in Japan, understanding the importance of gift-giving can help you establish strong connections with your Japanese colleagues and clients.

Gift-giving in Japan is deeply rooted in the country's culture, with centuries-old traditions. In Japanese culture, gift-giving is a way of expressing gratitude, respect, and appreciation for others. Giving gifts is also seen as a way to build and strengthen relationships, whether in personal or professional settings. Regarding business relationships, gift-giving is particularly important as it demonstrates a commitment to the relationship and a willingness to invest time and effort in maintaining it.

When giving gifts in Japan, it's important to remember the etiquette and cultural norms surrounding the practice. For example, gifts should be wrapped tastefully and should never be given in the presence of others. In addition, it's customary to include a handwritten note expressing gratitude and appreciation for the recipient. The gift should also be high quality and not overly expensive or flashy, as this could be seen as trying to buy favor or influence.

It's also essential to understand the different gifts appropriate for other occasions. For example, bringing back a souvenir or specialty item from the location visited is customary when returning from a business trip or vacation. Giving souvenirs shows you were thinking of your colleagues or clients while away and valued the relationship. However, it's important to note that the gift should be reasonable, as this could be inappropriate. Please keep in mind that in Japan, most souvenirs are food items. Avoid bringing back toys, magnets, and physical objects that take up space unless it is small.

Another everyday gift-giving occasion in Japan is the end of the year, or "Oseibo," when gifts are given to clients and colleagues to express gratitude for their business or partnership over the past year. Oseibo is also an opportunity to start the new year positively by reaffirming business relationships and setting the stage for future success.

In addition to expressing gratitude and appreciation, gift-giving in Japan also serves another vital purpose: creating a sense of obligation or indebtedness. When someone receives a gift, they feel responsible for reciprocating the gesture later, creating a gift-giving cycle that helps strengthen and deepen relationships over time.

As a foreigner working in Japan, it's essential to understand the cultural significance of gift-giving and participate in the practice thoughtfully and respectfully. Doing so can build stronger relationships with Japanese colleagues and clients and contribute to a positive and productive work environment. Remember, gift-giving is a formality and a meaningful way to express gratitude and build lasting relationships.

The Reciprocal Gift:

Understanding the importance of reciprocal gift-giving is essential to avoid offending and strengthen business relationships. In Japanese culture, gift-giving is seen as an act of respect, gratitude, and appreciation. It is a way to show that you value and acknowledge the other person's effort in the relationship. Therefore, it is vital to reciprocate with a gift of similar or greater value. Failure to do so could be seen as a lack of respect and appreciation for the other person's efforts.

Reciprocal gift-giving is a form of social exchange that builds trust and creates a sense of obligation between colleagues. By reciprocating a gift, you show that you value and are committed to maintaining the relationship. It creates a cycle of reciprocity, which fosters a sense of community and shared responsibility.

It is crucial to note that the value of the gift is not the most critical factor in this exchange. The act of giving and receiving is more important than the actual gift itself, and it is a symbolic gesture that reinforces the relationship and builds trust between colleagues. Therefore, putting thought and effort into selecting a gift that reflects your appreciation and respect for the other person is essential.

Reciprocal gift-giving is not limited to colleagues alone but is also a common practice between businesses, partners, and customers. It is a way to show appreciation for the business relationship and maintain loyalty. By exchanging gifts, companies can strengthen their ties and create a sense of community around their brand.

In conclusion, understanding the importance of reciprocal gift-giving is critical to navigating Japan's modern work culture. It is a way to show appreciation and respect and build trust between colleagues, businesses, and partners. Gift-giving is not a one-way street, and it is essential to reciprocate with a gift of similar or greater value. By doing so, you are strengthening the relationship and fostering a sense of community and shared responsibility.

Remember, the value of the gift is not as significant as the act of giving and receiving, so put thought and effort into selecting a gift that reflects your appreciation and respect for the other person.

Chapter Eighteen: Business Card Etiquette

Business card etiquette, or meishi-gire, is crucial to Japanese business culture. In Japan, a business card is not just a piece of paper with your contact information; it represents your identity, status, and professionalism. Giving and receiving business cards is essential to the initial introduction and sets the tone for the rest of the business relationship.

When presenting a business card, the proper way to do it is to hold the card with both hands, with the text facing the receiver, and bow slightly as a sign of respect. This gesture shows that you are giving the card with respect and humility. Similarly, when receiving a business card, it is polite to accept it with both hands, read it carefully, and then place it on the table before you. Putting the card away without looking at it is seen as disrespectful.

The information on the business card is also essential in Japanese culture. It should be written in English and Japanese, with the Japanese side facing up. The order of the information is also significant. The person's name should be written in large font and placed at the top of the card, followed by the job title and company name. The address, phone number, and email address are then placed at the bottom.

Keeping your business cards in a leather or plastic case is also essential. This case shows that you care about your cards' appearance and are serious about your business relationships. You should also never write on a business card in front of the person who gave it to you, as it is seen as rude and disrespectful.

In Japan, exchanging business cards is more than just a formality; it is a way to establish a relationship of trust and respect. By giving and receiving business cards with the proper etiquette, you show that you value the other person's time and effort and are serious about building a long-term business relationship. It is also important to remember that a business card is not just a contact information tool but also a representation of your company and brand.

Mastering the art of meishi-gire is essential for anyone who wants to succeed in Japan's modern work culture. By understanding and respecting the nuances of business card etiquette, you can establish yourself as a professional and build strong, long-lasting business relationships.

Remember always to present and receive business cards with respect, keep them in a proper case, and never write on them in front of the person who gave them to you. With these simple gestures, you can show that you are serious about your business relationships and that you value the culture and traditions of Japan.

Chapter Nineteen: Drinking Culture

Drinking culture plays a significant role in Japan's modern work culture, and foreign workers need to understand this aspect to thrive in the workplace. In Japan, drinking after work, or "nomikai," is a common practice and a way to build relationships with coworkers and clients. While some workplaces are different, being aware of drinking customs and etiquette is essential to navigating Japanese business culture successfully.

One of the primary reasons for the importance of drinking culture in Japan's modern work culture is the emphasis on building solid relationships with colleagues and clients. In Japan, relationships are highly valued, and bonding over drinks is seen as a way to break down barriers and form connections. It is common for Japanese business people to have several rounds of drinks after work or to attend a series of nomikai events to establish and maintain relationships.

Another reason drinking culture is so influential in Japan's modern work culture is the idea of "tatemae" and "honne." Tatemae refers to the face people present to others, while honne refers to their true feelings. In Japan, expressing one's true feelings is not considered appropriate, significantly negatively. Drinking provides a way to let down one's guard and express their true feelings in a more relaxed setting.

However, it is essential to remember that drinking culture can also be a potential minefield for foreign workers. In Japan, there is an unspoken rule that subordinates must follow their superiors' lead, which also extends to the drinking culture. It is common for senior employees to pressure their juniors to drink more than they can handle, which can lead to embarrassing situations or worse. Foreign workers must be aware of their limits and communicate them clearly to avoid misunderstandings.

There are several drinking etiquettes to follow in Japan's modern work culture. Firstly, waiting for a toast before taking a sip is essential. A common way to toast is by saying "kanpai," which means "cheers." Secondly, it is considered good manners to pour drinks for others, not oneself. Holding the bottle with both hands is essential as a sign of respect when pouring drinks. Finally, it is customary to thank the person who pours the drink by saying "arigatou gozaimasu." Please remember that you are expected to fill your colleagues' glasses if you see they are empty or near empty, especially if you are a new hire or a woman. If you are finished drinking, leave your glass half-full or more on the table, so no one tries to fill it.

In Japan's modern work culture, drinking culture is essential in building relationships and maintaining harmony. However, it is crucial to be mindful of one's limits and communicate them. By following drinking etiquette and respecting cultural customs, foreign workers can successfully navigate Japanese business culture and build strong relationships with colleagues and clients.

Drinking Parties and What to Look Out For:

Drinking culture is an essential aspect of Japanese work culture and can be a double-edged sword for foreign workers. While drinking with colleagues can be an opportunity to build solid relationships and networks, it can also be a potential source of tension and difficulty for those who are not used to the heavy drinking culture.

One issue that can arise from the drinking culture is peer pressure. In Japan, it is common to drink heavily, and toasting to colleagues is a regular occurrence. As a foreigner, it is essential to remember that excessive drinking can lead to poor performance at work and may even lead to health issues. While it is okay to participate in drinking with colleagues, it is essential to set boundaries and know when to stop. It is important to understand that saying "no" to drinks is okay if you have had enough.

Another potential issue is the need for more inclusivity. Drinking events are often considered a part of the team-building process, and those who do not participate may feel excluded. Drinking events can be challenging for those uncomfortable with drinking or who cannot consume alcohol for religious or health reasons. In such cases, it is crucial to communicate your concerns to your colleagues or managers and suggest alternative team-building activities that everyone can participate in.

Drinking culture can also be a barrier for women in the workplace. Women in Japan are expected to maintain a higher level of decorum and modesty, which can be a challenge when heavy drinking is involved. Women may feel pressured to participate in drinking events, leading to feelings of discomfort and potential health issues. In such cases, it is crucial to recognize women's unique challenges in the workplace and ensure that team-building events are inclusive and respectful of everyone's needs and preferences.

It is common for business associates to bond over drinks after work, and this practice has been in place for many decades. However, with time, the potential dangers of excessive drinking have become increasingly apparent. For a foreigner who wants to work in Japan, it is essential to understand the potential risks associated with the drinking culture in Japan's modern work culture.

The first potential danger is the pressure to conform to the group mentality. In Japanese culture, it is considered disrespectful to decline a drink when offered to you, mainly if it is from a superior. This pressure to conform can result in excessive drinking, leading to health problems, poor decision-making, and even accidents.

The second potential danger is the possibility of alcoholism. According to a study conducted by the Japanese Ministry of Health, Labor, and Welfare, more than one million Japanese people are believed to be suffering from alcoholism. The high level of alcohol consumption, coupled with the pressure to conform, can lead to addiction, which can severely impact both personal and professional life.

The third potential danger is the possibility of sexual harassment or assault. In recent years, several high-profile cases of sexual harassment and assault have been reported in Japan. Alcohol consumption can lower inhibitions and lead to poor decision-making, making people more vulnerable to these incidents. It is crucial to know how to handle such situations and clearly understand what constitutes harassment or assault.

The fourth potential danger is the impact on mental health. Drinking culture in Japan is often linked to the concept of "nomunication," or communicating while drinking. "Nomu" means "to drink" in Japanese. While this practice can be a way for people to connect and bond, excessive drinking can lead to emotional outbursts and arguments. For individuals struggling with mental health issues, excessive drinking can exacerbate their condition and harm their well-being.

It is crucial to understand that while drinking culture is essential to Japanese work culture, it is not mandatory. One can politely decline a drink and still maintain respectful relationships with colleagues, and setting boundaries and communicating openly and honestly with colleagues about limits and expectations is critical.

Prioritize your health and well-being above societal expectations. Drinking culture in Japan is deeply ingrained in society, but it should not come at the cost of one's health or personal values. Knowing when to stop, setting personal limits, and seeking help when needed can help mitigate the potential dangers of drinking culture in Japan's modern work culture.

Understanding the dangers associated with the drinking culture in Japan's modern work culture is critical for a foreigner who wants to work in

Japan. It is essential to recognize the pressure to conform, the possibility of addiction, the risk of sexual harassment or assault, and the impact on mental health. Setting personal limits, communicating openly with colleagues, and prioritizing health and well-being can help mitigate these potential dangers and ensure a successful and fulfilling career in Japan.

Chapter Twenty: Chopstick Etiquette

Understanding chopstick etiquette is essential to Japanese culture, particularly in the workplace. As a foreigner working in Japan, you must familiarize yourself with chopstick etiquette to avoid any unintentional social faux pas that could damage your reputation.

Unlike Western utensils, chopsticks are held using three fingers instead of two. The chopsticks should be held towards the end of the sticks with your thumb and index finger while the middle finger supports the bottom. It is also essential to avoid using chopsticks to spear or stab food, as this is considered rude.

In Japan, it is also customary to use different chopsticks for communal dishes, such as a shared hot pot or sushi platter. These communal chopsticks are provided for everyone and should not be used to pick up individual food portions.

Additionally, it is considered impolite to pass food directly from your chopsticks to someone else's chopsticks, as this is reminiscent of a funeral ritual in Japan when it comes to passing the remains after the cremation process. Passing food with chopsticks can also view it as being unsanitary and crude. There is a real emphasis on each person's food being personalized in Japan, even from a communal dish. Instead, using a communal serving utensil or placing the food on a person's plate is standard.

When you finish eating, returning the chopsticks to their original placement is essential. In most cases, this will be in a chopstick holder or wrapper provided by the restaurant. Leaving your chopsticks on the table or placing them in a rice bowl is impolite. Chopsticks standing in the rice in the bowl is reminiscent of another funeral ritual in Japan where you leave the dead something which brought them enjoyment when they were alive.

When dining with colleagues or clients, paying attention to their chopstick use and following their lead is essential. If someone offers you chopsticks or offers to pour you a drink, it is polite to accept the offer.

Finally, it is crucial to understand the significance of chopsticks in Japanese culture. In Japan, chopsticks are not just a utensil for eating but a symbol of refinement and grace. Therefore, treating chopsticks with respect and observing chopstick etiquette is a way to show respect for Japanese culture.

By familiarizing yourself with chopstick etiquette, you will show your colleagues and clients that you respect Japanese culture and are committed to building positive relationships in the workplace. It is a small but significant way to demonstrate your professionalism and build trust with your Japanese colleagues.

Chapter Twenty-One: Understanding Indoor and Outdoor Shoes

When working in Japan, it's essential to understand and respect the country's customs and etiquette. One of these customs that may seem unusual to foreigners is wearing indoor shoes or "wa-gutsu" in many workplaces and other public places. While this may seem small, it's an integral part of Japanese culture and can significantly impact your interactions with colleagues and overall experience working in Japan.

The tradition of wearing indoor shoes in Japan dates back centuries, and it is a sign of respect and cleanliness. It is believed that removing outdoor shoes and wearing indoor shoes helps to keep floors and other indoor areas clean, which is especially important in a culture where cleanliness is highly valued. Some Japanese homes and establishments have separate outdoor and indoor shoe areas; visitors are only sometimes asked to remove their shoes before entering.

In many Japanese workplaces, it is customary for employees to wear indoor shoes instead of outdoor shoes. Using indoor shoes is especially true in places like schools, hospitals, and other public buildings, where cleanliness and hygiene are vital. By wearing indoor shoes, employees can help to keep the floors clean and prevent the spread of germs and other contaminants.

If you're working in Japan, it's essential to understand the proper etiquette for wearing indoor shoes. In most cases, you will be provided with a pair of indoor shoes when you arrive at your workplace. These shoes are typically kept in a designated area, such as a locker or shoe cabinet. Keeping your indoor shoes clean and well-maintained is essential, as they reflect your hygiene and respect for Japanese culture.

Sometimes, you may be required to bring your indoor shoes to work. If this is the case, choosing a pair that is comfortable, easy to slip on and off, and appropriate for the workplace is essential. Avoid shoes with loud colors or patterns, and choose a simple and understated pair.

When it comes to wearing indoor shoes, there are a few important rules to remember. First, it's essential always to wear socks with your indoor shoes. Changing into your wa-gutsu helps keep your feet clean and prevents odors from building up inside the shoes. Additionally, you should only wear your indoor shoes in the workplace or designated indoor areas. Wearing your outside shoes indoors is rude and disrespectful, as they can track dirt and other contaminants.

Finally, it's essential to respect the traditions and customs of Japanese culture when it comes to wearing indoor shoes. While it may seem like a small detail, it is an integral part of Japanese etiquette and can significantly impact your relationships with colleagues and overall experience working in Japan.

Wearing indoor shoes in Japan's modern work culture is vital in respecting Japanese customs and etiquette. Employees can help keep floors clean and prevent the spread of germs and other contaminants by wearing indoor shoes. When wearing indoor shoes, it's important to wear socks, keep them clean, and never wear them outside designated indoor areas. You can respect Japanese culture and build strong relationships with your colleagues by respecting these customs.

Bathroom Slippers:

In Japan, it is customary to take off one's shoes before entering a home or office, and bathroom slippers are provided for use in the bathroom. This practice may seem odd to those unfamiliar with it, but it serves several vital purposes and is an essential aspect of Japanese hygiene culture.

The importance of bathroom slippers in Japan's modern work culture is rooted in several factors. Firstly, it is a way of maintaining hygiene standards. Japanese culture greatly emphasizes cleanliness, and wearing shoes outside the bathroom is considered unclean. The use of bathroom slippers ensures that the toilet remains clean and germ-free. Bathroom slippers are essential in a workplace where several people share the same bathroom.

Bathroom slippers are seen as a way of showing respect for others. In Japan, wearing the same shoes inside and outside the house is considered rude. By providing separate slippers for use in the bathroom, the employer shows respect for their employees' hygiene and well-being. This attention to detail is essential to Japanese work culture, emphasizing respect and hierarchy.

In Japan, it is essential to keep separate spaces separate. Using bathroom slippers ensures that the bathroom remains a particular space and is not contaminated by outside elements. Adhering to using bathroom slippers is a necessary aspect of Japanese culture, which values order and cleanliness.

Mindfulness in Japan is considered an essential aspect of daily life, and using bathroom slippers reminds one to be mindful of one's surroundings. By taking off one's shoes and putting on bathroom slippers, one is reminded to be present at the moment and to take care of oneself and one's surroundings.

In Japan's modern work culture, understanding the importance of bathroom slippers is essential for a foreigner who wants to work in Japan. Using the wrong slippers or not using them at all can be seen as a sign of disrespect or a lack of understanding of Japanese culture. It is, therefore, essential to follow the correct protocol when using the bathroom at work.

When entering a Japanese workplace, one must remove one's shoes and put on the provided indoor shoes. You should always wear these indoor shoes except when entering the bathroom. One should remove the indoor shoes and put on the provided slippers when entering the bathroom. It is important to remember that bathroom slippers are only worn inside the toilet and should not be worn outside.

When leaving the bathroom, one should take off the bathroom slippers and put them back in their designated place. One should then put back on the indoor shoes and continue with their day. It is important to note that you should never wear indoor shoes in the bathroom, which can be considered unclean and disrespectful.

Using bathroom slippers is not only a matter of hygiene but also a sign of respect for others and a way of maintaining boundaries and promoting mindfulness. Following the correct protocol when using the bathroom at work can show respect for Japanese culture and create a positive impression in the workplace.

Chapter Twenty-Two: Language Barrier Issues

The language barrier is a critical aspect of Japan's modern work culture that you cannot ignore. For foreigners who want to work in Japan, it is essential to understand the language, customs, and etiquette to build effective relationships with colleagues, customers, and partners. Please understand the nuances of the language to avoid misunderstandings, communication breakdowns, and missed business opportunities.

Japanese is a complex language with different writing systems, such as hiragana, katakana, and kanji. It is crucial to have a basic understanding of the language. While many Japanese businesspeople speak English, conversing in Japanese can help build deeper relationships and demonstrate a commitment to the culture.

One of the critical aspects of the language barrier in Japan's modern work culture is the use of honorifics, such as "san," "sama," and "sensei." These titles are used to show respect and deference to colleagues and superiors. Using the correct honorifics can be challenging for foreigners, requiring a nuanced understanding of the Japanese language and culture. However, failing to use them can be seen as disrespectful and could damage business relationships.

Another aspect of the language barrier is understanding non-verbal communication. In Japan, non-verbal cues, such as body language and facial expressions, are critical to communication. Understanding these cues is essential for effective communication and building relationships. For example, a lack of eye contact can be seen as a sign of disrespect or insincerity, while a slight bow can show respect and gratitude.

In addition to language and non-verbal communication, understanding cultural customs is essential when working in Japan. Japanese business culture significantly emphasizes building relationships and respecting colleagues and superiors. Understanding customs such as gift-giving, bowing, and hierarchical relationships is essential.

We discussed how gift-giving is an integral part of Japanese culture, particularly in business—exchanging gifts during business meetings or after a successful project is expected. However, gift-giving in Japan is not just about the gift itself but how it is presented. The gift-giving demonstrates respect and gratitude; wrapping and giving the gift is essential.

Understanding gift-giving customs can help build strong relationships with Japanese colleagues and partners.

Bowing is another essential custom in Japan's modern work culture. Bowing is used to show respect and gratitude, and different types of bows are used for different situations. Understanding the nuances of bowing can be challenging for foreigners, but it is essential to building relationships in the Japanese business world.

Understanding the hierarchy within a company is essential to know whom to address. It would be best to practice which honorifics to use and how to behave in different situations. Failure to understand the hierarchy can lead to misunderstandings and damage business relationships.

Understanding the language barrier is critical for foreigners who want to work in Japan's modern work culture. It is essential to have a basic understanding of the Japanese language, customs, and etiquette to build effective relationships with colleagues, customers, and partners. Please understand these nuances to avoid misunderstandings, communication breakdowns, and missed business opportunities. By understanding the language and culture, foreigners can build solid relationships and succeed in Japan's modern work culture.

Japanese Uses About a Third More Onomatopoeias than English:

Understanding the sounds expressing ideas, feelings, and experiences is essential to understanding the Japanese language and culture. They are used extensively in daily Japanese conversations, advertisements, and workplaces. These words mimic sounds and actions, making them an effective way to convey meaning and emotions.

In the Japanese language, onomatopoeias are called "giongo" (擬音語) and "gitaigo" (擬態語). Giongo refers to sound effects, while gitaigo describes actions, emotions, and other non-auditory phenomena. For example, "pikapika" represents sparkling, and "guruguru" represents spinning. Many onomatopoeias in Japanese can describe almost anything, from the weather to food and feelings and emotions.

In Japanese work culture, understanding onomatopoeias is essential as they express various emotions and situations, including politeness and respect. For instance, when greeting someone, it is common to say "ohayou gozaimasu" (おはようございます), which means "good morning." However, to show extra respect, one can say "ohayou gozaimashita" (おはようございました), which has a different tone and conveys a deeper level of respect. This subtle difference in language can make a big difference in building positive relationships with colleagues and superiors in the workplace.

Onomatopoeias are also used in everyday conversations and to describe different situations in the workplace. For example, "gacha gacha" (ガチャガチャ) is the sound of something being locked or closed. In an office setting, it describes the sound of a closed filing cabinet or someone typing on a keyboard. Understanding these onomatopoeias is essential for a foreigner working in Japan as it helps them to communicate better with colleagues, understand their emotions, and respond appropriately to different situations.

Onomatopoeias are also used in Japanese advertising and marketing, an essential aspect of Japanese culture. The use of onomatopoeias in advertising and marketing is to convey emotions and feelings, making them more relatable and appealing to the audience. For example, a car commercial may use the onomatopoeia "zum zum" to represent the sound of a car engine in Mazda commercials, creating an emotional connection with the audience.

Onomatopoeias are essential to Japanese culture and business language. Learning onomatopoeias can help build positive relationships with colleagues, understand their emotions, and respond appropriately to different situations. Onomatopoeias are also used in advertising and marketing, making them an essential aspect of Japanese culture in the workplace and beyond.

Chapter Twenty-Three: Major Japanese Holidays to Know

New Years:

The Japanese New Year, or shogatsu, is one of the most important holidays in Japan's modern work culture. It is when people take a break from work and spend time with their families, reflecting on the past year and looking forward to the future. As a foreigner who wants to work in Japan, understanding the significance of shogatsu and its customs can help you to navigate Japanese work culture more effectively. Think of Japanese New Year as Christmas for the west.

Firstly, it is crucial to understand that shogatsu is a time for renewal and starting fresh. Many businesses close down for several days or even a week, so planning your work schedule is essential. You may need to get your work done before the holiday, or you may need to delay it until after the holiday. Either way, it's essential to communicate effectively with your colleagues and clients to ensure understanding.

Shogatsu is a time for giving gifts, or oseibo, to colleagues, clients, and business partners to show appreciation for their support throughout the year. If you are working in Japan, it is vital to understand the customs around gift-giving, such as the appropriate types of gifts and the proper way to present them. As explained previously, gift-giving can help you to build stronger relationships with your colleagues and clients, which is essential in Japanese work culture.

Shogatsu is also a time for eating traditional Japanese food, such as ozoni (a soup with mochi), osechi (a special kind of bento), and doboroku (Japanese unfiltered or homSupposerewed sake). Suppose you are invited to a shoga celebration. In that case, you must be familiar with the customs around eating and drinking, such as the proper way to use chopsticks and the appropriate amount of sake for drinking. You can demonstrate your understanding and appreciation of Japanese culture by respecting these customs.

During shogatsu, people reflect and set intentions for the new year. Many Japanese people visit shrines and temples to pray for good fortune and success in the coming year. As a foreigner in Japan, it can be helpful to participate in these customs to show respect for Japanese culture and to set your intentions for the new year.

Shogatsu customs are essential to navigating Japanese work culture as a foreigner. By planning your work schedule accordingly, understanding gift-giving customs, respecting traditional food customs and setting your intentions for the new year, you can demonstrate your understanding and appreciation of Japanese culture and build stronger relationships with your colleagues and clients.

Golden Week:

Golden Week is a collection of national holidays in Japan observed in late April and early May each year. For foreign workers who want to work in Japan, it is crucial to understand Golden Week and its customs as it affects the country's work culture. Golden Week is one of the busiest times of the year in Japan, with millions of people traveling domestically and internationally. Therefore, knowing about this period and its impact on the workplace is essential.

Golden Week is a collection of four national holidays, which include Showa Day on April 29, Constitution Day on May 3, Greenery Day on May 4, and Children's Day on May 5. Due to the proximity of these holidays, many Japanese workers take off the period between these holidays to create an extended vacation. Many Japanese workers highly anticipate the Golden Week period as it provides a rare opportunity for a prolonged break from work.

For foreign workers who want to work in Japan, it is vital to understand the customs surrounding Golden Week. Many businesses and companies close during Golden Week, meaning foreign workers should plan their work schedules accordingly. However, some businesses and industries, such as hospitality, travel, and retail, remain open and are even busier than usual during this time. As a result, foreign workers in these industries should expect to work more during the Golden Week period.

It is also important for foreign workers to be aware of the impact of Golden Week on transportation and other services. Due to the large number of people traveling during this time, public transport is often crowded, and many popular tourist destinations can be overcrowded. Using public transit during peak holidays can make travel and commuting challenging for foreign workers, and they should be prepared for long travel times and delays.

In addition to understanding the impact of Golden Week on work schedules and travel, foreign workers should also be aware of the customs and traditions associated with this period. For example, many Japanese people use Golden Week to visit family and friends or travel domestically or internationally. It is common for people to exchange gifts during Golden Week, particularly on Children's Day, which is a traditional time for families to celebrate the growth and happiness of children.

In the workplace, it is common for employers to give employees a bonus or a gift during Golden Week as a way of showing appreciation for their hard work. This gesture is often viewed as a way to maintain positive relationships between employers and employees and to motivate workers to continue working hard.

By being aware of the impact of Golden Week on work schedules and travel and understanding the customs and traditions associated with this period, foreign workers can better navigate the challenges and opportunities of working in Japan. They can also show respect and appreciation for the culture and traditions of their Japanese colleagues, which can help build strong and positive relationships in the workplace.

Obon:

Obon is a traditional Japanese holiday in mid-August and is one of Japan's most important cultural events. Understanding Obon and its significance in the country's modern work culture can be very helpful for a foreigner who wants to work in Japan. In this essay, we will explore the importance of Obon and how it affects the workplace while also providing insights on navigating this holiday as a foreign worker in Japan.

Obon is a time when Japanese people return to their hometowns to pay respect to their ancestors and deceased loved ones. It is believed that during this period, the ancestors' spirits returned to the living world to visit their families. For this reason, Obon is often called the "Festival of the Dead" or the "Festival of Souls." Obon lasts three days, during which people visit their ancestral graves, hold family reunions, and participate in traditional events such as Bon Odori dancing.

Obon is a significant event for Japanese workers because it is when many people take a break from work to visit their hometowns and spend time with their families. Many businesses close during Obon, and some employees take a week or more off. For foreigners unfamiliar with the culture, this can come as a surprise, and they may need help understanding the significance of the holiday or why it is so important to take time off work. However, it is essential to respect this tradition and know that it is an integral part of Japanese culture.

Being aware of Obon and how it may affect your work schedule is crucial as a foreigner working in Japan. Some businesses may close for the entire week, while others may only be closed for a few days. It is essential to check with your employer beforehand to understand how your company handles this holiday and whether you will be expected to work during this time. It is also essential to plan accordingly and arrange any necessary time off or travel plans.

One of the most significant events during Obon is the Bon Odori dance, a traditional folk dance performed during the festival. This dance is performed to welcome the spirits of the ancestors and is a significant part of the holiday. As a foreigner, you may have the opportunity to participate in this dance, and it is a great way to experience Japanese culture and connect with your colleagues.

Obon is also when many Japanese people give their families and friends gifts. This tradition is known as "Ochugen," It is customary to give gifts of food or household items to express gratitude and appreciation. As a foreigner working in Japan, it is vital to understand this tradition and show respect by giving gifts to colleagues and bosses. It is also important to note that Ochugen gifts are not expected in the workplace, but they can be a nice gesture to show appreciation.

Obon is a time when many businesses close, and employees take time off to visit their families and pay respect to their ancestors. As a foreign worker, respecting this tradition and planning for this holiday is crucial. By showing respect for this holiday and participating in traditional events such as the Bon Odori dance and giving Ochugen gifts, you can demonstrate your appreciation for Japanese culture and strengthen your relationships with your colleagues and bosses.

PART V: Conclusion

Understanding the cultural nuances and practices in Japan's modern work culture is critical for foreigners planning to work there. These practices can seem unfamiliar or even strange to outsiders, but they are essential to creating successful working relationships and integrating into Japanese society.

The Wa, or the importance of harmony, should not be taken lightly. Understanding the concept of collectivism in Japanese culture and how it affects the workplace is crucial. Individuals are expected to put the group's interests before their own, which can lead to decisions being made slowly, as everyone's opinion is considered. However, everyone must work towards the same goal once a decision is made.

Honne and Tatemae deal with the difference between what someone truly thinks and what they say or do. Indirect conversation can confuse foreigners, as it is not always easy to tell when someone is honest or hiding their true feelings. Understanding this difference is critical to building trust with coworkers and creating successful relationships in the workplace.

The Fear of Failure can also be a significant issue for foreigners working in Japan. The pressure to succeed and maintain a good reputation is incredibly high, and mistakes are not taken lightly. However, failure should be seen as an opportunity to learn and improve, not as a reason for punishment.

Japanese Hierarchy is an essential aspect of the work culture. Understanding where you fit into the hierarchy and respecting those above you is critical. It is also important to remember that respect is earned in Japan and is not given freely based on job title or position.

Sempai is a term used to describe someone senior to you in the workplace. Respect for sempai is essential, as they are seen as role models and mentors. However, it is also important to remember that sempai is not infallible and can make mistakes.

Company Contracts in Japan are usually much more comprehensive than in other countries. Understanding the terms of your contract is critical, as they will govern your employment and benefits.

Arrangements can also include provisions for overtime work, which is expected in many Japanese companies.

The Japanese work culture is a unique and complex system that has evolved over centuries. The importance of punctuality, the emphasis on teamwork, and the need for consensus are crucial aspects of this culture. Understanding and respecting these norms is vital for success in the workplace.

Work Culture Norms You Should Know Beforehand include various practices, such as bowing, gift-giving, and chopstick etiquette. These practices may seem insignificant, but they are an essential part of Japanese culture and can significantly impact how you are perceived in the workplace.

Working in Japan as a foreigner can be both challenging and rewarding. By understanding and respecting the cultural practices and norms of the Japanese work culture, foreigners can create successful relationships with coworkers and thrive in their new work environment. It is crucial to approach these differences with an open mind and a willingness to learn, as this will help you to integrate into Japanese society and build a fulfilling career.

About the Author

Brian Takahashi is an American living and working in Japan for over a decade. During his time in Japan, he has worked in various industries, including management, tourism, and education. With his extensive experience in the Japanese work environment, he has gained a deep understanding of the cultural differences and challenges of working in Japan.

Brian is also married to a Japanese woman with two children. His personal experiences have given him a unique perspective on Japanese culture and family life, which he has shared with others through his writing and speaking engagements.

As a bilingual speaker of English and Japanese, Brian has bridged the communication gap between Japanese and non-Japanese coworkers and clients. He has also used his language skills to volunteer as a translator for various community events and organizations.

Brian's passion for Japan and its culture has led him to become a respected member of the ex-pat community in Japan. His insights and knowledge about life and work in Japan have been valuable to those considering living or working there.